MW00960060

The Walker Boys

Adventure Series Book 3

BIGFOOT

BY JESS WALKER

ILLUSTRATED BY PRADIPTA MUKHERJEE

DEDICATION

To my wife Julia, the love of my life and soulmate. Your unwavering support has reignited my passion for writing.

CONTENTS

The Stanley Cup Final

The score is 2-2. It's a tied game with only one minute left in regulation time. It's the Stanley Cup Final, and the Toronto Maple Leafs are close to winning it all! Morgan Walker has the puck behind his net. He looks up at the scoreboard and sees the clock ticking down: fifty-nine, fifty-eight, fifty-seven...

He looks down the ice and sees a flash of blue rocketing past him. It's Marshall Walker! Morgan passes the puck to him,

1

and it hits the tape of his stick! Marshall is off!

He tightropes his way along the sideboards, zigzagging and weaving through a wall of defenders. Thirty-five, thirty-four, thirty-three... the seconds tick by. This is the most exciting Stanley Cup Final anyone has ever seen. The fans are on their feet, chanting, "Go Leafs, go! Go Leafs, go!

Marshall skates past center ice. Then, a player on the opposing team comes out of nowhere. He's built like a tank. He steamrolls toward Marshall at breakneck speed, not slowing down but speeding up. Marshall looks up and sees number 77 inches away from him. The crowd falls breathlessly silent, waiting for the bone-crunching hit—but none comes.

Marshall jukes to the right and does a spin-o-rama around number 77, narrowly missing the hit. He spots Max Walker, wide open and heading to the net. He slings a laser-tight pass to Max, who gets the puck on his stick. He is all alone! There are only ten seconds left! The fans count down with the clock: "Ten, nine, eight, seven..."

Max fakes a slap shot. The goalie goes down to stop the puck, but there is no puck. Max has it on his stick with a wide-open net. The goalie tries to scramble back, but he's out of time. The puck launches off Max's stick, pings off the iron, and flies into the empty net!

He shoots, he *scores!*" yells the announcer. "The Toronto Maple Leafs have won the Stanley cup!"

"Max, wake up! Get out of bed, we're late!"

The screaming fans and the hockey arena disappear. It was only a dream. How could it not be a dream being the Toronto Maple Leafs. Opening his eyes, Max sees his younger brother, Morgan, hovering over him. He looked at the alarm clock beside his bed. It was blinking 12:00 AM.

"The storm last night shut down the power. "That's why we all slept in late," explained Morgan.

"And that's why we're about to be late to the big game if we don't get a move," insisted Marshall, the youngest of the three Walker boys.

4

He picked up a pillow off Max's bed and tossed it at him.

"Hey!" grumbled Max. "That was too hard!" He whipped the pillow back at Marshall but missed.

Marshall made a face at him.

Max turned to Morgan. "What time is it really?"

Morgan looked down at his watch and frowned. "It's nine o'clock, and our game is in half an hour!"

Max jumped out of bed. "We have to leave now, or we'll be late for our game! We know what the coach is like. He'll bench us for sure!"

Morgan and Marshall hurried to their bedrooms to get changed. Max already had his pants and socks halfway-up.

The boys knew what was at stake. It was the final game of the season, and it was a must-win. If they lost, they wouldn't make the playoffs. The Wilmington Wild Cats would be itching at the chance to beat them!

A minute later, they were in the kitchen, bundled up in their winter gear with their hockey bag packed and ready to go. Mrs. Walker had toast and jam waiting for them on the counter. She had slept late too and felt terrible for not getting them out of bed on time. She grabbed her car keys and hurried to the front door. "You better eat in the car. I'll drive you."

Nobody followed her out—she was forgetting something important.

"Why are you standing there and staring at me. Let's go!" she insisted.

Marshall had to point out the obvious.

"But Mom, you're still in your bathrobe and slippers. There's two feet of snow outside, and it looks really cold."

She looked down and blushed. "I knew I'd forgotten something. Just wait here, I'll go get changed," she said, hustling up the the stairs.

Julia Walker was always busy and on the go, never doing one thing but multiple things at any given time, which often resulted in her forgetting something. This week was no exception. Last week, she couldn't find her car keys, and the week before that, she misplaced her laptop.

Max knew if they waited any longer, they'd be late. He also knew their mom took forever to get ready in the morning. They would have to get there on their own.

Five minutes later, Mrs. Walker came back downstairs. There was no sign of the boys. Instead, she saw a note on the door that read, 'See you at the arena. Found another way to get there. XOXO.'

Mrs. Walker stared out the window and wondered how they were going to get to the arena if not by car. She had a feeling this was just the beginning of another Walker Boys Adventure!

Safety Tips & More
Dreams: page 118

Bunker Hill

The boys sat on a sled and surveyed the hill below. It was sunny without a hint of a cloud, but a slight breeze came in from the north that chilled them to the bone. It hadn't taken them long to get there, because the hill sat directly behind their house on the other side of the fence.

Max sat at the back and held onto the rope, ready to steer. Morgan was in the middle, and Marshall was cramped in the front.

Bunker Hill was a massive hill that stretched as far as the eye could see, past a landscape dotted with snow-covered evergreens and pockets of farmers' fields. At the bottom of the hill sat the arena, the place they had to get to fast. They marveled at the winter wonderland around them. Everything was blanketed in a foot of snow.

How the hill got its name was a subject of great debate. Legend had it that an underground bunker was hidden somewhere on the hill and stored inside was enough gold to fill up the entire Whitebush Hockey Arena.

Morgan exhaled deeply and saw the vapor from his breath cloud around him like steam from a kettle against the cold air. He moved his fingers around the inside of his mitts to warm them up.

"I can't feel my hands. I think they're frozen," he moaned.

"That's not the only thing frozen," declared Marshall. "I can't open my eyes. My eyelashes have frozen shut."

Max had to one-up them all. "You think that's bad? My nostril hairs are frozen together. I have to breathe through my mouth, and the air burns going down because it's so cold."

Max pushed off, and the sled lurched ahead as they began their descent down Bunker Hill, gradually building up speed with each passing second. The sled kicked up a spray of snow in the cold moving air, stinging their faces like tiny pinpricks and making their eyes water.

An old wooden farmer's fence appeared in the distance, surrounded by a thick entanglement of needled trees and bare bushes and vines on the other side.

Max didn't turn left or right but went straight on a collision course with the fence.

Morgan was beginning to get worried. "You're not turning! We're going to hit the fence!" he warned.

Max didn't answer because he was too focused. Stopping was no longer an option.

The fence was suddenly on them and only a few feet away—but instead of hitting it, they went right through it. There was a narrow gap in the fence no wider than the sled itself. The sled burst through, then bulldozed over a mesh of vines and bushes.

Next came the trees. Max pulled the rope left and right, weaving around tree after tree like a snake through grass. Finally, they broke clear and entered a field full of kids, all doing what kids do best: playing! Some were sledding, others were building snowmen, and a few more were enjoying a good old-fashioned snowball fight.

Morgan looked at his watch and frowned. "We only have seven minutes!" he shouted.

"We're almost there," Max reassured him.

He kept the sled on a straight path toward the arena. Nothing was going to stop them now—he felt sure they were going to make it on time. Or were they? Suddenly, a kid in a bright red snowsuit on a one-person sled cut right in front of them. Max wasn't so sure anymore!

He yanked the rope hard, and the sled swerved out of the way, just missing the kid but sending them on a new path—not toward the arena, but to the outer edge of the hill that disappeared down a steep ravine into the woods below.

When they hit the edge of the hill, they were catapulted into the air like a pebble from a slingshot.

It happened so fast that nobody had time to react as they soared past the tops of pine trees! Morgan's survival instincts kicked in. He unwrapped his scarf from around his neck and held it out with one hand.

As the sled brushed past the top of another pine tree, he shot the scarf around it like a lasso going around a bull's neck.

When the scarf hooked on, he held on tight and swung the sled around the tree in the opposite direction, landing them back safely on the hill.

Just when they thought they were in the clear, another obstacle appeared out of nowhere. This time it was large, white, round, and menacing. It gazed at them with an evil stare. Its eyes were black and ominous, and completely unforgiving. There was nowhere to go because it was on them. It was them against it!

Safety Tips & More
Bunkers: page 120

BIGFOOT

The Headless Snowman

It was a snowman! They were going to hit it for sure! The two kids who were putting the final touches on the snowman looked up in surprise. They dove out of the way just before the sled hit a bump and went airborne, plowing into the head of the snowman, knocking it clean off.

Their snowman was now a headless snowman! The two kids looked around for the head but couldn't find it. That's because it was now planted firmly on top of Marshall's head!

When more kids further down the hill looked up and saw a snowman on a sled, speeding their way, they panicked.

"Look!" one kid yelled. "That snowman is trying to run us over!"

"Run for your lives!" shouted another kid. "He's going to get us!"

A sea of different colored snowsuits scrambled out of the way just before the Walker Boys shot past them.

"I can't get the head off!" cried Marshall. "It's stuck on my head!"

"I can't see anything!" complained Max. "The head is in the way."

"Let me try to get it off," insisted Morgan.

He grabbed the head with both hands and tugged at it until it popped off, sending it sailing through the air, before it landed and began to roll. It continued to roll down the hill, picking up more snow along the way, growing bigger and faster with each rotation.

Marshall was surprised that the snowman's head didn't break apart when it hit the ground. "That thing is like a bowling ball! It can't be broken."

"Forget a bowling ball," stammered Morgan, "try a wrecking ball!"

"You're both wrong," interrupted Max. "It's now the size of mom and dad's minivan!"

"And it's headed straight for the arena!" hollered Morgan.

Kids dodged out of the way, narrowly missing the giant rolling snowball careening past them.

Three older kids stood at the base of the hill, directly in its path. But with their backs turned, they were unaware that they were about to be plowed over.

"Get out of the way!" yelled Max.

"Move!" shouted Morgan.

The three older kids didn't move because they never heard them. It was too late—a second later, the giant snowball steamrolled over top of them, flattening them into the snow, face-first like a pancake! The giant snowball didn't stop there, but continued to roll into the parking lot, where it hit the opposing team's parked bus and crumbled into a heap of powdered snow.

The Walker boys were only seconds behind and on the same collision course. Max yanked the rope to turn, but it broke. He no longer could steer the sled! The only direction they could go was straight—the same path the giant snowball had just taken.

A smile creased Marshall's face when the three older kids looked up. He recognized them, and by the looks on their faces, they recognized him and were none too pleased to see him! The feeling was mutual.

They were the two mean teenagers and Lorenzo Duke, the town bully. They'd had plenty of run-ins with them in the past, and the bad blood between them was still strong. One of the teenagers was Lorenzo Duke's older brother—the spitting image of Lorenzo, but bigger and uglier!

Before they could get out of the way, the sled hit them, knocking them down like bowling ball pins.

"Strike!" shouted Marshall as the sled bull-dozed over top of them.

Shouts of anger could be heard behind them. "We're going to get you, Walker Boys! This isn't over!"

Max and Morgan recognized the voices. When they looked behind to confirm their suspicions, they weren't surprised. They no longer felt bad about the collision!

The sled bounced onto the parking lot, flying past parked cars and people making their way toward the arena. The parking lot was like a skating rink, and the slick ice was making them go much faster. The snowplows had come and cleared the snow, but not the ice underneath!

"Who needs an arena when you have a parking lot?" yelled Max. "The ice is perfect!"

"Close to perfect, except for the parked cars," said Morgan.

"And moving cars!" pointed Marshall. "Like the one backing up right now that doesn't see us coming!"

With no way to steer and the sled gaining speed, something needed to be done before it was too late!

"Quick, Morgan, open the hockey bag!" shouted Max. "I have an idea that might just work, and I'm in the perfect position to try it!"

Safety Tips & More
Road Safety:
Page 122

The Grand Entry!

Max yelled in Morgan's ear, "Quick! Pass me a hockey stick and a skate!"

Morgan turned and looked at him like he was crazy but did it anyway. Max stuck the skate on the end of the hockey stick. He positioned the hockey stick behind him and used it like a rudder for a boat. The skate dug into the ice and carved a line behind them. Max pulled the hockey stick toward him, and the sled veered left, just missing the reversing van.

Max kept the sled in line with the double-door entrance to the arena, which was fast approaching. He couldn't stop the sled, but he could turn it, and the double-door entrance was better than a brick wall!

The only problem was the doors were closed!

"Somebody, open the door!" boomed Marshall.

"Move out of the way!" warned Morgan.

Two things happened at once. People scrambled out of the way, and the door swung open just before the sled swooshed inside, skidding over the cement floor of the main lobby in a shower of sparks.

The sled came to a screeching stop at the end of the hallway, against a familiar pair of black leather boots tapping impatiently against the cement floor.

They looked up and weren't surprised to see their dad, Mr. Walker, who was also the team's coach, standing in front of them!

Jess Walker was always at the arena an hour before games and practices, and today had been no different, snow and all!

He looked down at his watch and frowned. "You guys are a minute late."

Nobody bothered to respond. After everything they had been through to try and make it on time, they were still late, even if only by a minute!

Then a big smile lit up his face. "Just kidding. Do you think I would be upset that you're a minute late? Especially after the big dumping of snow we got! I'm just glad you made it!"

Morgan rolled his eyes, and in his most unimpressed voice, said, "Good one, Dad. You got us there, ha-ha."

"Yeah, real funny, Dad," crowed Marshall, pretending to smile.

Mr. Walker walked past them and made his way to the main lobby. "The game's delayed by twenty minutes, so you guys have plenty of time to get ready. I'll see you on the ice. I'm going to go check out the collection."

"What collection?" asked Max.

Mr. Walker stopped and turned.

"You haven't heard?"

"Heard what?"

"If you get ready on time, maybe you'll get a chance to see it before the game starts." He half-smiled as he turned and walked on.

"You guys know what Dad's talking about?" asked Max.

"Not a clue," replied Morgan

"I got nothing," said Marshall.

A familiar voice from behind them answered their question. "It's a hockey card collection."

They turned to see their good friend, Jerry, standing behind them with his little sister, Janie, along with a kid they'd never seen before.

"And it's not just any ordinary hockey card collection," declared Jerry. "It has the Wayne Gretzky and Mario Lemieux rookie cards in it."

"Wow!" exclaimed Max. "Those cards have to be worth a fortune!"

"They're priceless if you ask me," remarked Jerry. "Worth too much money to sell."

"Forget about the cards," said Janie. "I'm just glad nobody got hurt, especially you, Marshall." She walked over and gave him a big hug, followed by a kiss on the cheek.

Marshall blushed.

Right on cue, the teasing began. Max started to sing the dreaded song. It was the same song he had sung the last time Janie showed her affection toward Marshall. It drove him crazy.

"Marshall's got a girlfriend, Marshall's got a girlfriend, Marshall's got a girlfriend!"

Marshall elbowed him hard in the stomach.

"Ouch! What was that for?" howled Max.

Marshall didn't say anything but gave him the *don't mess with me* look.

Max knew that look. He'd seen it plenty of times before—it meant *keep it up at or else.* "Okay, okay little brother, I'm just joking around."

When Marshall got mad, nobody wanted to be on the receiving end. He was affectionately nicknamed *The Bruiser* by his brothers.

Sensing the growing tension, Jerry changed the topic. "This is my little cousin, Bobby. He's staying with us for a week."

Janie whispered to Marshall, "It's going to be a long week. So far, he's almost set the house on fire and taken our dad's car for a joyride."

"Greetings, Earthlings," announced Bobby in his best alien voice. "I am Zodar from the planet Pling-Plong." He waddled around with his feet out and his head bobbing up and down like a chicken.

"I forgot to mention," warned Jerry, "Bobby thinks he's an alien."

Bobby said nothing and continued with his alien act down the hallway, going from a walk to a full-out sprint.

Jerry took off after him. "Get back here, Zodar—I mean Bobby—whatever your name is!" he shouted.

Janie waved goodbye and chased after Jerry.

Morgan couldn't help but grin. "Jerry's going to have his hands full with that little rug rat!"

"And we're going to have our hands full if we're not ready to play in twenty minutes," Max reminded them.

They hurried inside the change room, where they were high-fived by their teammates, who were beyond happy to see them because now they stood a chance of winning! Ten minutes later, with their skates tied, helmets strapped on tight, and equipment buckled down, they were ready to play.

Max was the first out the door. Before he could take another step, he heard somebody cry out for help! It sounded like Jerry, and it was coming from the ice rink. Morgan and Marshall heard it, too. They took off down the hallway, through the swinging doors, and onto the ice rink. They were shocked at what they saw next!

Safety Tips & More
Anger: page 123

5

Zamboni on the Loose!

It was Bobby, and he was driving the Zamboni! Jerry was on the ice chasing him. The crowd looked on as Bobby drove left, then right, in circles, and then in zigzags around the ice. He looked like he was having the time of his life, grinning wide and laughing at Jerry, who was only a couple steps behind him trying to catch up.

Jerry looked winded as he yelled in-between breaths, "Bobby! Get back here! Push the brakes to stop the Zamboni!"

Bobby heard him and giggled. He knew exactly where the brakes were but chose to push the accelerator instead to go even faster!

Jerry always did a weird thing whenever he ran, and he was doing it again—his tongue was hanging out the side of his mouth like a panting dog! The watching crowd couldn't help but notice, and some people even laughed. A couple of seconds later, Jerry's tongue proved to be more of a danger than a five-year-old driving a Zamboni.

Jerry lunged at the Zamboni, and at that same instant, the Zamboni braked suddenly, causing him to crash headfirst against the side of it. He should have bounced off, but he didn't. Instead, he clung to it—not by his hands, but by his tongue! His tongue was latched onto the cold metal of the Zamboni like paper stuck to glue!

The situation had just turned from bad to ugly.

Max said to Marshall. "Get the Shooting Star from the hockey bag. I think we're going to need it."

Seconds later, the Walker boys were on the ice, skating after the Zamboni. Jerry managed to grab a hold of something to keep from being dragged by his tongue. When Bobby saw his new chasers, he did something nobody expected.

He drove straight out of the arena! He didn't stop there but continued to drive through the parking lot and toward the road! Water continued to spray out the back of the Zamboni while the compressor smoothed out a path of perfect ice.

The Walker boys stuck close behind, skating hard to keep up. When Bobby turned and saw them, he pushed the accelerator down until it wouldn't go any further. The Zamboni picked up more speed. He was going fast! Faster than fast! So fast that they could no longer keep up with him.

Bobby stuck out his tongue and taunted them. "Can't catch me!"

They were losing him, and Max knew something needed to be done before it was too late. He pulled out the Shooting Star. It was a gold-plated device no bigger than the palm of his hand and shaped like a chalk brush. A star-shaped object was attached to the end of it.

He aimed and fired, and a split second later, a star shot out, dragging a cord behind it. His aim held true, as the star wrapped around a metal pole near the back of the Zamboni.

"Quick, grab on to me!" hollered Max.

Morgan and Marshall latched onto Max, and Max gripped the end of the Shooting Star. Now they were being dragged behind like a water skier

being pulled by a boat, except it was a Zamboni, and they were on ice skates, not water skis!

Marshall looked ahead and saw what was coming next. "You better hold on tight, we're about to hit the road!"

When they turned onto the road, they kept going straight until the cord yanked them in the new direction.

The next obstacle was fast approaching and blocking the middle of the road. It was clearly visible to them all, including Bobby. But instead of slowing down, he pushed his foot down harder! He was going to hit it!

Safety Tips & More
Zambonis: page 125

BIGFOOT

6

Close Call!

I t was a police car blocking the road, and its flashing lights and siren were going off at full blast. A police officer stood in front, waving his arms to stop. He looked familiar. Max knew they had to stop the Zamboni before it was too late. That's where the Shooting Star came in.

"Here we go!" he warned. "Hold onto me and don't let go!"

He pushed a button on the Shooting Star and the cord retracted, pulling them toward the Zamboni until they were close enough to climb on board. Max was the first one on and the first one to get to Bobby. When he got there, he plucked Bobby from the seat and sat down to take over the controls. He slammed on the brakes, and the Zamboni skidded to a stop. He stood up and looked for the police officer but couldn't see him over the hood of the Zamboni. Fearing the worst, he scrambled off with Bobby in tow to have a look. Morgan and Marshall followed.

When he got there, he saw that it was Officer Rodriguez, and he didn't look happy! He said one word to them: "*explain.*"

Max looked down at Bobby. "Our little friend here thought it would be funny to take the Zamboni for a ride," began Max. "We were there when it happened at the ice rink, and we chased him all the way here."

"And luckily for you, we stopped him just in time," explained Morgan.

Officer Rodriguez looked down at Bobby and frowned. "And you must be Bobby. When I got the call, I thought it was a prank, but you just proved me wrong, son."

"My name isn't Bobby, it's Zodar, and you have just taken over my spaceship. I will get revenge, Earthling!"

"Well, Zodar, I come in peace, but I'm sure Momma and Poppa Zodar won't be as peaceful after they're through with you."

Max handed Bobby over to Officer Rodriguez, who put him in the back of his cruiser.

He smiled and shook his head slowly. "You Walker boys are like magnets to danger. Wherever you go, danger is always close behind, but somehow, you always manage to defeat it."

"Thanks in large part to you," suggested Morgan.

"You're right," agreed Marshall. "Who can forget the one-armed man in the cave or the crazy cat man on the boat you saved us from?"

The officer let out a soft chuckle. "I remember those two wild adventures you went on, and I have a feeling your third adventure may have just begun!"

"What makes you say that?" asked Max.

"The call that came into the police station also reported that a rare hockey card collection was stolen."

The boys blurted out at the same time, "Somebody just stole a Wayne Gretzky and Mario Lemieux rookie card!"

Officer Rodriguez was just as shocked. "I'm going to find the culprit responsible for this. In my opinion, those are the two best hockey players of all time!"

Morgan had to set the record straight. "You mean *we* have to find the culprit—as in, you, me, Max, and Marshall.

"You can help, but try to be safe doing so," he reminded them.

"Just for the record," added Marshall. "Tie Domi is one of the best hockey players of all time. He was small but mighty, and he used his fists to do all the dirty work."

"I wouldn't expect anything different from The Bruiser himself," laughed Morgan. "Who, I might add, has a Tie Domi rookie card worth a whopping two dollars."

Everybody except Marshall laughed. Even Bobby, who was sitting in the cruiser, had a good belly laugh.

Their laughter was cut short when a strange sound broke in.

"What's that awful sound?" asked Officer Rodriguez.

The boys looked at each other and shouted, "We forgot about Jerry!"

They hustled to the side of the Zamboni, where they found poor Jerry still holding on by his fingertips and tongue!

"Wow!" exclaimed Marshall. "I never knew your tongue was that long, Jerry. It looks like it belongs to a lizard, not a human."

Max tried to keep a straight face. "Now isn't the time for one of your bad jokes, Marshall... even if his tongue is a little tied up and he can't talk," he smirked.

Jerry tried to respond, but only got a few mumbled words out that nobody understood.

Officer Rodriguez gestured at the others. "I've got just the thing to get Jerry's tongue free. I'll get it from my cruiser."

When he returned, he had a warm cup of coffee in his hand. "I sure hope that you like coffee, Jerry." He leaned in and slowly poured the coffee over his tongue until it ripped free.

"Ouch!" cried Jerry. "That hurt!"

"Oh, great, he can talk again," kidded Morgan. "There's no stopping him now."

Jerry didn't look impressed. "Real funny, Morgan! And yes, I can talk, so you're going to have to put up with me whether you like it or not! I can't feel my tongue, and it feels like my taste buds have been ripped out because I can't taste the coffee, which is probably a good thing, I suppose."

"They're likely still on the side of the Zamboni," teased Marshall.

Officer Rodriguez's patience was wearing thin. "Who is looking after Bobby, and where are his parents?"

Jerry looked up, a little embarrassed. "I was looking

after him, but not very well, as you can see. His parents are down visiting for the week. They're staying at my house. That's where they are right now."

"Then that's where I need to take him," decided Officer Rodriguez.

"We'll need a lift to the arena first," said Jerry. "My little sister Janie is there, and the Walker boys have a hockey game to play."

Officer Rodriguez looked at the Walker boys, in their skates, helmets, and hockey equipment, and half-smiled. "I kind of figured that out already."

He turned and headed for the cruiser. "Everybody, get in."

Jerry gave Officer Rodriguez his parents' address as he pulled up to the arena to drop them off.

Before they got out, Max had a couple of questions to ask Bobby.

"Bobby, what made you take the Zamboni... I mean, the spaceship, for a ride?"

Bobby pulled a five-dollar bill out of his pocket to show Max. "He gave me this if I'd do it, so I did it."

"You mean take the spaceship for a ride?" asked Max.

"Affirmative," replied Bobby in his best robot voice.

"Who exactly gave you the money? What did he look like?" asked Max.

Officer Rodriguez listened intently.

"He had blue eyes and long white hair. He wore a cowboy hat with matching boots. His boots looked like they belonged to a clown because they were so big."

"Like how big?" asked Max.

"This big." Bobby stretched his arms wide and showed him.

"That's big," agreed Max. He turned to Morgan, Marshall, and Jerry. "Time to go."

When they got out of the cruiser, they saw Janie waiting for them. Officer Rodriguez rolled down his window, "I'll be back, right after I return our alien friend to his parents."

Jerry was relieved to see Janie, although it looked like Janie was more relieved to see Marshall than her older brother. She had a wicked crush on Marshall and wasn't afraid to show it. She walked over to him and gave him another hug, this time longer and harder.

"I can't breathe!" gasped Marshall. "You're squeezing too tight."

Janie let go and frowned.

Marshall felt bad, "Sorry Jannie, I didn't mean to upset you."

Janie shook her head. "It's not that Marshall. There's something else I need to tell you guys and I'm afraid it's bad news. The hockey game has been cancelled."

The Walker boys weren't surprised at all to hear the news. Even though they were disappointed, they shrugged it off. Hockey would have to wait. Find the missing hockey cards was their top priority.

Jerry spoke next. He confirmed what everybody else was already thinking. "I think the cowboy is the one who stole the cards."

"It sure looks that way," agreed Morgan.

"The Zamboni was meant to be a distraction. While everybody was watching Bobby, nobody was watching the hockey cards."

"And that's when he must have stolen them," concluded Max.

"Which would have been the easy part," suggested Marshall. "Nobody was there to stop him."

Janie looked puzzled. She glanced over at her big brother. "Why did you call the suspect a cowboy?"

"Because he's dressed like one. He's got a hat and boots to prove it. Really big boots, I've been told."

What Janie said next got everybody's attention. Unexpectedly, they got their first big clue!

Safety Tips & More
Emergencies:
page 126

The Crazy Cowboy

I saw him! Blurted Janie. "He was walking up Bunker Hill."

"Are you sure it was him?" asked Max.

Janie thought about it before she answered. "He was far away, and his back was turned to me, so I didn't get a good look at him, but he was wearing a cowboy hat and boots. That much I know for sure."

"I think it's a good chance it was him," said Morgan. "How many people do you see wearing a cowboy hat in the middle of winter?"

"Nobody," answered Marshall.

"Except for him," finished Jerry.

"If his feet are as big as clown feet, he'll leave behind prints in the snow that we're sure not to miss," added Max.

"Which should lead us right to him," confirmed Morgan.

"What are we waiting for, let's go!" urged Marshall.

Max waved them on. "Let's head back to the locker room and get out of our hockey gear. Walking on skates up a hill would not be a smart thing to do."

Five minutes later, they returned to the same spot where Jerry and Janie were waiting. Morgan carried the Shooting Star, and Max wore his new gadget that he was excited to try.

Jerry made it abundantly clear that he was going with them, whether they liked it or not. Janie, on the other hand, had different ideas. The last thing she wanted to do was chase a crazy cowboy around Bunker Hill. She was going to stay behind and wait for Officer Rodriguez to return. She had a feeling they were going to need his help.

The Walker boys and Jerry began their search. The hill looked even busier than before, crowded with kids. It didn't take them long to find what they were looking for. Marshall waved them over to have a look.

When they got there, they were shocked at how big the boot prints were!

"Maybe he is part Bigfoot," suggested Morgan. He stuck his foot inside and laughed. "My foot looks like a baby's in comparison."

Jerry couldn't help himself. "Your foot isn't the only thing that's like a baby. Sometimes you act like one, too." He rubbed his eyes and pretended to cry like a baby, "Waah, waah! I'm Morgan. Waah, I want my milk!"

Morgan scowled at him. He never liked it when he was a punch line for one of Jerry's jokes.

Everybody jumped when a voice from behind them cut in. "Hey, dweebs, remember us?"

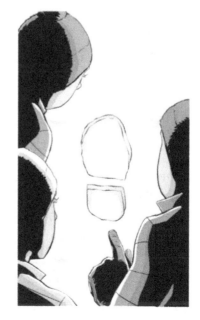

They spun around to find Lorenzo's older brother, his sidekick, and of course, Lorenzo Duke himself.

Their faces were swollen and bruised.

Jerry spoke first. The boys held their breath, knowing exactly what was coming. Jerry had a way with words that easily got under other people's skin. He didn't disappoint this time around.

"It looks like you guys just got run over by a milk truck." He paused for effect and then spoke again. "Oh, wait a minute, you *did* get run over—but it wasn't by a milk truck, it was by a sled with the three Walker boys on top."

Lorenzo's face reddened, and the veins on the side of his neck began to bulge. "You guys are the ones that are about to be run over, and it's going to be by our fists"

Jerry didn't stop there. He kept on talking. "I would say your faces, which are already ugly to begin with, just got a whole lot uglier. If there was an ugliest face competition, the three of you would win first, second, and third prize."

He looked at Lorenzo's brother. "You would take first, obviously."

Lorenzo's brother glared at him. He took a step forward.

"I wouldn't take a step further," warned Jerry. "Morgan here has his black belt in karate."

During their last adventure, he had said the same thing to the bullies. It looked like they didn't forget as they approached with caution.

"I do?" Morgan asked.

"Sure, you do," replied Jerry.

"He'll make quick work of the three of you," warned Jerry.

"I will?" asked Morgan.

"Sure, you will," answered Jerry.

Morgan whispered to Jerry, "Are you trying to get me beat up? Because if you are, it's working."

Jerry put his arm around him. "Relax, Morgan. You always have an answer for most things. This time should be no different, right?"

Morgan wasn't impressed. "Jerry and his big mouth," he muttered.

Max and Marshall gave him a concerned look.

"What did you just say to me, Mr. Black Belt?" asked Lorenzo's brother.

"Nothing," Morgan shot back. "I like to talk to myself."

"Well, you're going to be talking to my fist in a second."

Both Lorenzo and his brother's sidekick laughed. They all took another step closer. Jerry eased behind Morgan to hide. Max and Marshall stepped beside him.

Morgan had to think fast before things got out of hand. Thoughts raced through his mind as he wondered what to do next, and then it hit him. He knew what to do! It was crazy, but it might just work!

Safety Tips & More
Bullies: page 129

Charge!

Morgan placed two fingers in his mouth and let out a long, loud whistle that could have shattered glass. All the kids playing on the hill stopped what they were doing and looked his way. They weren't going to like what he was about to say, even if it was a tiny lie.

He pointed at Lorenzo's brother, his sidekick, and Lorenzo himself and yelled, "These three bullies told me that they're planning on taking over the hill and stealing your sleds!"

72

An awkward silence filled the air. The hordes of kids who were laughing and playing moments ago weren't doing so anymore. They looked like a pack of starved wolves about to launch a full-out attack.

The bullies backed up slowly. "That's not true!" shouted Lorenzo. "Morgan is making that up!"

Lorenzo was right—Morgan *was* making it up, but the kids on the hill didn't know that, and even if they did, they wouldn't have cared. He was Lorenzo Duke, the town bully, the one who always made other kids cry.

To speed things along, Morgan shouted one more thing that sealed the bullies' fate. "Oh, and they also said you guys are a bunch of snot-nosed little crybabies."

The silence was suddenly broken by a boy in a bright-blue snowsuit screaming,

"*Chaaarge!*"

And just like that, a mass of kids ran at them from all directions, until the bullies were cornered and had nowhere to go. A second later, the kids pounced on them, piling on top of them until they were buried beneath a growing mound of swinging arms and flying fists.

Morgan marveled at the sight before him. "Looks like justice has been served."

"And you didn't even have to raise a finger," declared Jerry.

"Let's go find Bigfoot," announced Max.

Jerry couldn't help but laugh. "For our sakes, I hope he isn't Bigfoot. We'll be in big trouble. Get it, *big* trouble?" He emphasized the word to make his point.

Morgan rolled his eyes. Jerry always came out with a corny joke at the worst time. "Whatever, Jerry."

They made their way up the hill, following the same path they had taken earlier on their sled. When they were halfway up, the trail of boot prints disappeared into the woods on the far side of the hill.

They followed the tracks into the woods but froze halfway when something jumped out at them. It was big and black and white and furry, and headed their way!

Jerry gave a high-pitched shriek, and Max and Morgan turned to run, but Marshall didn't seem to care. He had eyes like an eagle and knew they had nothing to worry about. Why? Because it was Baxter, the dog, and once again, he was off his leash.

Baxter jumped up on Morgan and licked his face. Mr. Barber, Baxter's owner, came running behind. "I'm sorry, Morgan. Baxter, get down!"

Morgan laughed as Baxter continued to lick his face. "That's okay, Mr. Barber, I don't mind. I love dogs."

"What brings you boys out here?" Mr. Barber asked. "Don't you have a hockey game to play?"

"We did, but something bad happened," explained Max, "and we're trying to fix it."

The older man nodded like he'd heard it before—and because it was the Walker boys, he had. "It sounds like another one of your wild adventures."

Marshall grinned. "I suppose you could call it that, with a little bit of craziness and danger in the mix too."

"You didn't by chance walk by anyone wearing a cowboy hat and boots?" asked Max.

Mr. Barber paused to think about it. "I only passed one person on my walk, which isn't unusual out here. And I do believe he was wearing a cowboy hat," he chuckled. "I didn't see his boots because the snow was covering them. Baxter didn't seem to like him much—he growled at him on the way by."

Jerry cleared his throat. "Speaking of Baxter, isn't that him over there running down the hill?"

Mr. Barber was already on the move again, chasing after him. The boys set off, this time with more urgency in their step.

The trees seemed to swallow them up, the deeper in the woods they hiked, until there was no sunlight left, only a light shade of green. The whistling of the wind and the crunching of their boots were the only sounds they could hear. It was quiet—too quiet. And then it happened. All four of them froze in their tracks.

"Are you seeing what I'm seeing?" sputtered Jerry.

Nobody said a word. They just stared.

Safety Tips & More
Winter Navigation:
page 131

BIGFOOT

It was Bigfoot! He looked part ape and part man, covered from head to toe in a tangle of unruly, matted brown hair. His feet were colossal, and his hands looked like giant paddles.

The boys crouched down and watched with a mix of fear and curiosity. Morgan couldn't believe his eyes. He had read about Bigfoot and the sightings made by countless people across the world claiming to have seen him. But all of them were just that: claims. Hard to believe, and maybe true.

Now he believed it! Bigfoot wasn't made up. He was real because he was looking right at him!

"What's he doing?" whispered Jerry.

Max was just as confused. "If you ask me, it looks like he's out for a leisurely walk in the woods."

"Bigfoot doesn't walk in the woods," interrupted Morgan. "He *hunts* in the woods. Wherever he goes, he looks for food, especially meat."

"Like kid meat," added Jerry

Morgan ignored him. "It's said that he has an incredible sense of smell and can smell just about anything from miles away."

Marshall made a face. "Speaking of smells. What is that smell?" he said, plugging his nose.

Max and Morgan smelled it, too.

Jerry knew the answer because he was the one who made it. "Sorry, that was me. Whenever I get nervous, I *fart*."

"Ahh, Jerry," complained Marshall. "Put a plug in it."

Morgan suddenly realized something. They were in more danger now because of Jerry. This time around, his butt cheeks had done the talking, not his big mouth. Trouble was on its way—all three-hundred pounds of it!

"If we can smell it, then Bigfoot can, too," advised Morgan.

And smell it he did, because seconds later, he turned in their direction and ran. He was headed their way like a heat-seeking missile locked onto its target!

"Run!" hollered Max.

They turned and ran like their life depended on it because it did! If Bigfoot caught them, it would be game over! Trees flashed by, and branches whipped at their faces as they hustled through the woods.

Max looked behind and saw that they were out-running Bigfoot. His huge feet were slowing him down. Just when things were beginning to look up, they took a sudden turn for the worse. Max saw the whole thing unfold.

Jerry fell face-first into the snow. When he got up to run, he couldn't, because his leg was stuck between two smaller trees. Morgan and Marshall looked on in shock as Bigfoot caught up to him. The fearsome creature stood over Jerry and let out a triumphant cry that made the hair on the back of their necks stand straight up!

"What do we do now?" asked Morgan. "Do we leave Jerry behind or pick a fight with Bigfoot?"

Fearless Marshall didn't answer—he was already halfway there, charging at Bigfoot and screaming at the top of his lungs.

"I guess we'll pick a fight then," muttered Morgan. He joined the charge with Max beside him and crazy Marshall out front.

The next thing that happened surprised everybody. They were expecting a fight for the ages, but they never got one because Bigfoot turned and ran!

"That's right, you better run!" shouted Marshall, pumping his chest.

When they got back to Jerry, they were relieved to see that he wasn't hurt, although he was beyond scared.

Jerry pried his one eye open. "Is he gone?" he whimpered.

"He's gone," Marshall reassured him. "One look at me and he made a run for it."

Morgan rolled his eyes. "You do know we were right behind you?"

"Whatever," countered Marshall in his best 'I don't care' voice.

Max looked down at Jerry. "Let's get you out of this mess, shall we?"

Morgan crouched down and untangled Jerry's leg from the tree and Max helped him to his feet.

Jerry asked, "So why did Bigfoot run? I know Marshall said it was because of him, but that's hard to believe, isn't it, all four-foot nothing of him?"

"Hey," warned Marshall. "I'm standing right here, you know."

Max said, "If you ask me, the only thing that scared him off was your *fart.* If

Bigfoot's sense of smell is that good, he must have really smelled that one."

Morgan tried hard not to laugh. "With farts as smelly as yours, we'll have to start calling you *Jerry the Fartinator.*"

"Real funny," sneered Jerry. "At least I'm still in one piece and not his dinner."

"I think his dinner would have been spoiled if he ate you," laughed Max.

Jerry shrugged it off. "Besides my fart, I did notice something weird about him. But if I tell you, you're going to think I've gone crazy."

"We already know you're crazy, but tell us anyway," said Marshall.

"I could have sworn I saw a price tag sticking out of his arm. And not only that, I think he was wearing blue underwear."

Morgan couldn't tell if Jerry was being serious or not. "If he was wearing underwear, don't you think we would have seen it, too?"

Jerry shook his head. "I didn't see all of his underwear, only the elastic band part that goes around the waist."

Max suddenly figured it out.

He looked at the others and asked, "When people wear loose-fitting pants, what do you sometimes see?"

"Underwear," answered Marshall.

"And Bigfoot had the same thing going on," hinted Max. "His pants were part of his costume!"

"So, somebody was dressed up as Bigfoot!" exclaimed Marshall.

"That explains the price tag," agreed Morgan.

Jerry was still confused. "So, what you're saying is that Bigfoot was wearing a Bigfoot costume? How is that even possible?"

Morgan was losing his patience. "No, Jerry. A *person* was wearing a Bigfoot costume to scare us off, and I bet it was the crazy cowboy."

"What are we waiting for, let's go!" shouted Marshall.

They hiked on, and soon found what they were looking for, but not what they were expecting—in fact, Jerry almost tripped over it!

Safety Tips & More
Bigfoot: page 135

The Bunker

Ouch! cried Jerry. He had just tripped and fallen face-first into the snow again!

"I feel like this has happened to you before," smirked Marshall.

Jerry ignored him and looked down at what made him trip. It looked to be some kind of hatch door and sitting on top was a rusted metal wheel with knobs sticking out.

The others saw it too and couldn't believe their eyes!

"The legend of Bunker Hill must be true," croaked Morgan. "The crazy cowboy must live in the bunker below."

"If it *is* a bunker," cautioned Max. "It could be anything."

"Whatever it is, the trail of footprints stops here, so he's got to be down there!" Jerry pointed out.

"Agreed," said Max. "And there's only one way to find out." He paused and took a deep breath, "That's to go down there."

Max twisted the wheel. The hatch opened with a muffled screech. He looked inside and saw a ladder descending down a dark tunnel. He felt for his new gadget—a wristwatch that served many different functions, one of them being a flashlight. He pushed a button, and a beam of light cut through the darkness.

Max climbed onto the ladder. "Try not to make a sound. If he hears us, he'll know we're here, and who knows what might happen next."

Jerry felt a lump in his throat. "For our sakes, let's hope the crazy cowboy really isn't crazy. Being stuck in an underground bunker with a crazy person isn't my idea of fun."

"That is if he *is* the crazy cowboy," countered Morgan. "Maybe he's Bigfoot and we're wrong about the costume."

Max began his climb down. Marshall went next, followed by Morgan and then Jerry.

When they got to the bottom, they hunkered down to have a look around. They were in a room no bigger than a closet.

Ahead of them lay a narrow cement corridor, which led to a dimly-lit room at the far end. Max tiptoed ahead, signaling for the others to follow. When he reached the room, he took a quick peek inside. He didn't see the crazy cowboy, nor did he see any gold. He saw something else that made his head spin. The others saw it too!

The entire room was jam-packed with hockey cards, pinned onto the wall and ceiling like it was wallpaper and packed into boxes scattered across the floor. The label on the boxes read, 'Bigfoot Hockey Cards: We're Big about Hockey.'

Morgan started to connect the dots. "I get it," he whispered. "The crazy cowboy is the owner of Bigfoot Hockey Cards, and the machine over there proves it," he pointed.

The others gazed at what he was pointing at. It looked like any household printer except that it held blank trading cards instead of paper.

Morgan didn't stop there. "The bunker must be his base of operations, where he makes the cards and stores them."

Jerry was confused. "If that's the case, why would he steal the Wayne Gretzky and Mario Lemieux hockey cards if he makes them?"

Morgan was one step ahead of him. "Because he doesn't make all the hockey trading cards out there. He steals them. As you said before, cards like that don't have a price tag—they're too valuable to sell."

"I wonder where he got the money to buy, sell, and make all these hockey cards?" asked Jerry.

Eagle-eyes Marshall already knew the answer because he could see it. He pointed at the opposite wall. "Look over there and tell me what you see."

"A wall plastered with hockey cards," answered Jerry.

"Look closer," urged Marshall.

Max's eyes lit up. "I think I see it. Are those gold bars I'm looking at?"

"Stacks of them," answered Marshall. "Most of them are hidden underneath the boxes."

Morgan and Jerry saw it too.

"Wait a minute," said Jerry. "Let me see if I understand this correctly. The crazy cowboy is the one who discovered the bunker and the gold inside. Then he used the money from the gold to buy hockey cards and make his own hockey card trading company, Bigfoot Hockey Cards.

"That about sums it up," agreed Morgan.

"So, any hockey card that wasn't for sale by the owner, he stole," said Max.

"Exactly," answered Morgan, "and if anybody got too close to the bunker, he wore the Bigfoot costume to scare them off."

Suddenly, the wall shook, and the whole bunker started to vibrate. It lasted only a handful of seconds before it stopped.

"What was that?" asked Morgan.

Jerry raised his hand. "Sorry, that was me again, except this one made a loud sound."

"You farted again!" hissed Marshall.

Morgan glared at him. "Really, Jerry?"

"Like I said before, I fart when I get nervous," he answered back.

"Speaking of getting nervous, you're about to get ten times more nervous," blurted Max. "Look who's coming!"

It was the crazy cowboy, and he was headed their way!

"Let's get out of here!" yelled Max

"Move it!" shouted Morgan

"Run!" hollered Marshall.

Flrpppppppp!" boomed Jerry, as he let another one rip.

Morgan was the first one to make it to the ladder. He scurried up, with Max, Marshall, and Jerry right behind. When he reached the top, he jumped out. Max and Morgan came next—but there was no Jerry.

The boys stared at each other with dread in their eyes. Max initiated the flashlight and shone it down the ladder. He saw Jerry, but he wasn't where he was supposed to be. He was barely hanging on—and not even by his hands!

Safety Tips & More
What is a Fart?
page: 137

11

Run!

Jerry was hanging upside down on the ladder! The only thing holding him up was his shoelace.

Max signaled to Morgan. "Get the Shooting Star out and aim it at Jerry's free leg."

Morgan pulled it out, aimed, and fired. The star shot down and hit Jerry's leg, wrapping around it in a knot.

"Got him!" yelled Morgan. He felt like he was fishing and just got a big bite, except it was Jerry at the other end of the line, and he was fifty times heavier!

It was a good thing Morgan fired when he did because a second later, the crazy cowboy grabbed hold of Jerry's arm.

He tried to pull him down, but luckily, the shoelace and the cord from the Shooting Star kept him up.

"Jerry! Let another one rip!" yelled Marshall. "That'll get him off you in a hurry!"

Jerry's face was beet-red from hanging upside down. "You want me to fart, Marshall?" he yelped incredulously. "I can't just turn it on and off like a light switch, you know!"

"You're going to have to make it happen if you plan on getting out of here!" Marshall called back.

Max's finger hovered over a different button on his watch. He waited for the right moment. "Jerry cut one loose!"

Jerry didn't disappoint. This one was even louder than the last. The crazy cowboy's face turned green as he let go of the shoelace.

At that same instant Max pushed a different button on his watch. A laser shot out and sliced through the shoelace, freeing Jerry from the ladder.

A second later, Morgan activated the Shooting Star and the cord retracted, reeling Jerry up until he was close enough to grab. Marshall got a hold of him and pulled him to safety.

Max slammed the hatch closed and spun the wheel until it wouldn't turn anymore. He knew that it could open from the inside, so he did the next best — he grabbed a large fallen branch and wedged it into the wheel so it wouldn't turn. He knew it wouldn't stop him from getting out, but it would slow him down enough so they could make a run for it.

The boys got to their feet and ran! Needled tree branches whipped at their faces and their outstretched arms as they navigated their way back. When they reached the hill, they stopped to have a look around.

"Do you see him?" asked Jerry.

Everybody looked at Eagle Eyes Marshall.

"I don't see anything, but I do hear something," he answered.

The others heard it, too. It was a faint rumbling sound that was getting louder. It sounded like a motor. Something was approaching them, and it was coming at them fast!

Then they saw him. It was the cowboy hat that gave him away. He was riding a snowmobile.

They ran down the hill, half-stumbling and half-falling, their feet not able to move fast enough. The sound of the snowmobile grew louder. Max looked over his shoulder, and he was right behind them! Almost on them!

Max shouted a last-second warning. "He's going to run us over!"

Everybody dove out of the way and waited for something bad to happen, but nothing did. When Max looked up, he saw the crazy cowboy headed for the woods with Officer Rodriguez in hot pursuit on his police snowmobile.

Max gave a big whoop at their good fortune. He thought about everything that had happened that day: the crazy sled ride, the wild Zamboni chase, the stolen hockey cards, spotting Bigfoot, Jerry's thunderous fart, and finally, almost getting run over by a snowmobile. It was too much for his brain to absorb.

Safety Tips & More
Stranger Danger:
page: 139

12

Take Him Away, Boys

When they made it to the bottom of the hill, they saw police officers and news reporters swarming around the arena parking lot. The first person to greet them was Janie. She ran up to them.

"I'm so glad you're okay and not hurt!"

"Thanks," said Jerry.

Janie scolded him. "I didn't mean you. I meant Marshall."

Max, Morgan, and Marshall couldn't help but laugh.

They looked past Janie and saw Officer Rodriguez handing over the crazy cowboy to two his fellow officers. "Take him away, boys."

He turned to face the kids. "You did it again, Walker boys. Another epic adventure and another case solved!"

Jerry shot him a dirty look. "Oh, and you too, Jerry."

Marshall reached into his pocket and reluctantly handed over the Wayne Gretzky and Mario Lemieux rookie hockey cards. "I managed to take these just before we got chased."

Officer Rodriguez took a second to admire the cards before handing them over to another officer for safekeeping.

"I have something for you, too," he said in return. "I'll take you back up there later. It's some kind of gadget, and I know how much you boys love your gadgets."

Officer Rodriguez went to speak again but stopped. His face suddenly turned green.

"What is that awful smell?" he asked.

"There's only one person I know who can turn somebody's face green," announced Morgan. He looked over at Jerry. "I thought you said you fart when you get nervous?"

"That's true," confessed Jerry. "But what I didn't tell you is that I also fart when I'm dog-tired. And that's exactly how I feel right now," he grinned.

Everybody plugged their noses and laughed, including Jerry!

–The End–

Safety Tips
& More

Dreams

Bunkers

Road Safety

Anger

Zambonis

Emergencies

Bullies

Winter Navigation

Bigfoot

What is a Fart?

Stranger Danger

Dreams

Have you ever had a dream about being a professional athlete or doing something really cool?

If you said yes, you're like most people. Dreams are what fuels the mind, brings passion to our lives, and drives us to do and accomplish more.

You can do anything you set your mind to, and don't let anyone tell you different! How do you think the car was invented, or the television or iPad for that matter?

One answer: it started with a dream.

Famous hockey players like Wayne Gretzky and Connor McDavid had a dream at a very young age to play in the NHL.

What separates them from others?

They both took massive action to become an NHL hockey player, and I'm sure, experienced many bumps along the way, but they stuck with it! It's called perseverance.

Dreams only remain dreams if you do nothing about them. Only when you take action can you work on achieving them. These are called goals. If you don't try, you'll never know what could have happened if you did. It's better to live a life full of oh-wells than one full of regrets. What would have happened if I......?

Bunkers

Bunkers are shelters located underground that people use to protect themselves or hide from danger. Bunkers are made of concrete and steel which is durable and hard to break, especially when under attack by enemy soldiers!

Soldiers used bunkers during WWI, WWII, and other wars to protect themselves from enemy bombs and bullets. In the 1960's during the Cold War, when Russia and the U.S. were at the brink of nuclear war, many families built underground bunkers in their own backyards.

Bunkers can vary from simple structures (a hole in the ground) to something more elaborate, like a home away from home. A kitchen, bedroom, living area, ventilation system, and let's not forget the washroom

120

are some of the features.

Next time you go for a walk outside, you may be walking over a bunker without even knowing it!

Road Safety

When you're walking in a parking lot, it's important to be extremely aware of the cars and people around you. If a vehicle is backing up, wait for it to reverse before you continue to walk. Many drivers fail to see kids behind them when they're backing up because they're not paying attention, or the poor kid just isn't tall enough to be seen!

If you see a car starting up or idling, there's a good chance it may be on the move. This is when you must be super alert and keep at a safe distance. Walk with an adult, and never run!

Anger

Marshall has quite the temper, which can sometimes get the better of him! When we get angry, we may do or say things we'll later regret. It's okay to feel an emotion, whether it's happy, sad, mad, nervous—you name it. What's not okay is when you deal with your emotions in a way that could put yourself or others in danger. Everybody has been mad before. If you haven't, you must be part robot! What do you do when you get angry?

The next time you get angry, here are some things you can try:

☐ Walk away

☐ Breathe deeply

☐ Count to 10

☐ Meditate

☐ Talk about it

☐ Write in a journal

☐ Do a physical activity that's healthy for your body (like using a punching bag instead of a person)

☐ 24-hour rule: before you say or do anything, leave it for 24 hours (a full day) before you respond. This will give you time to think about it and calm down before you act.

Zambonis

A Zamboni is an ice re-surfacer machine that clears all the loose snow and skate marks from the ice to create a smooth, bump-free surface.

Before the Zamboni was invented, by a man by the name of Frank Zamboni (no surprise there), it wasn't uncommon to see a team of up to three workers re-surface the ice the old-fashioned way—through hard work and sweat, using buckets of water, a wheelbarrow, sponge-brooms, and shovels. It took up to 90 minutes compared to today which is under 10 minutes thanks to the Zamboni!

Emergencies

What would have happened had Max not stopped the Zamboni on time? Officer Rodriguez would have been injured, perhaps severely.

Have you ever been in an emergency that required the police, fire, or ambulance? if you have, I'm sure you must have been scared!

What do you do if you find yourself in an emergency without an adult present? The short answer is, it depends. Every situation is different (a house on fire, somebody hit by a car, or a heart attack, to name a few), but here are some tips that might help:

☐ STAY CALM. I know, I know, this is much easier said than done. However, take a couple of deep breaths to try to calm yourself down.

☐ CALL 911. Talk slowly and clearly, and tell the operator what happened and where you are. The more you can tell them, the more prepared they will be when they arrive.

☐ STAY AT THE SCENE and provide help where you can before the professional help arrives.

The What Ifs:

There are a lot of what-ifs that I'm sure you're thinking about right now, like:

- ☐ What happens if I don't have a phone?

- ☐ What happens if I'm also injured?

- ☐ What happens if I'm on the roof of a speeding train? (I don't know about that one, but hey, why not.)

These are all different scenarios that require you to keep a level head and use common sense. Sometimes, the best solution is the simplest one.

Bullies

When a bully confronts you, sometimes the best thing to do is walk away or ignore them. The more attention you give them, the more they will continue to bully you. If you show fear, they'll hone in on you like a shark to blood. Stay calm and walk away.

Remember to use WITS:

☐ Walk away

☐ Ignore

☐ Tell someone

☐ Seek help

Are all bullies named Butch or Biff, with a short-cropped haircut, bushy eyebrows, and muscles rippling out of their shirt? *No.*

They can be anybody. The most innocent-looking person can be a bully!

Always remember, you're never alone if you're being bullied. There are always people out there who can help you and set things straight! It can be a teacher, a parent, a friend, a relative, a coach, a principal, anybody. So don't be shy! All you need to do is tell somebody and help will come! Always remember, there are different kinds of bullying. Just look below:

Winter Navigation

Have you ever gone for a walk or a hike on a really cold day? If you live in an area that has four seasons (summer, winter, spring, and fall), I'm sure you have. You know the feeling when you're freezing? Your fingers and toes go numb, it hurts to breathe (because the cold air burns going down), you might shiver, or even worse, your nose hairs and eyelashes stick together, just like in the story.

What must you do to stay warm?

Without pointing out the obvious, dress in winter attire. This includes a hat, gloves, scarf, and boots, among other things.

If you're doing physical activity outside, you might sweat. You want to avoid this (especially if you're far away from your home)! If you feel like you're overheating or might be sweating, take a layer of clothing off. When you stop moving, you no longer have your internal oven going (your body temperature), which keeps you warm. Your sweat will cling to your body and absorb your internal heat like a sponge, leaving you feeling chilled to the bone. I've been there before and done that. Not an enjoyable experience, but I did learn from it, and it's never happened again!

Are you going for a hike somewhere?

☐ Get permission from your parents first and tell them where you're going and when you expect to be back. If you have a phone, take it. If something terrible happens and you need help, your parents are only a phone call away.

☐ Take a real map. Yes, I said real—as in, you can hold it, feel it, and fold it. Use it as a backup so that you're not solely relying on a phone if that's what you are using. It's great when it's working, but what happens when you no longer have a signal, or your battery dies?

☐ Don't be afraid to get outside, especially in the winter! Just be smart about it and dress according to the weather conditions.

Bigfoot

There have been numerous accounts across the world of people claiming to have seen Bigfoot. Some sightings were hoaxes, such as people dressed up or images manipulated somehow to look like Bigfoot, while other sightings weren't made up—or so the evidence would suggest. You be the judge. What do you think? Is Bigfoot real or made up?

Sasquatch and Yeti are other names people have called Bigfoot, depending on where in the world it was spotted. The first sighting of Bigfoot was said to have been made in and around the coastal areas of California, Oregon, Washington, and British Columbia.

The next time you go camping and see a big ape-like creature standing almost seven feet tall covered from head to toe in an unruly mass of hair, you could be looking at Bigfoot! Then again, it might be a shadow, a bear, a moose, or even just your own imagination playing tricks on you. Who knows?

What is a Fart?

A fart is a bodily function that expels excess gas from your stomach through, you guessed it, your rear end. Burps are the same, but they go through your mouth. When you eat food, the acids in your stomach work hard to digest it, breaking it down into energy. Gasses sometimes get trapped when this happens and have nowhere to go but up or down!

Farting is normal, and everybody does it, even the queen of England. It's said that on average, a person farts 10-18 times in a single day.

When and where you fart is what you must be careful of. It's called having manners! For the next family get-together, when everybody is crowded in the same room, think twice before you let one go—instead, go somewhere private like the bathroom!

Stranger Danger

Was it smart for the Walker boys and Jerry to chase down a stranger? Of course not!

This is what the police are for: to uphold the law and enforce it on those who break it. They should have waited for Officer Rodriguez to return. Instead, they went ahead on their own and faced plenty of danger in doing so. This sure makes for a good story, but it's not smart in real life!

There are plenty of bad people out there who have done bad things to kids. Many of them are strangers, but not all of them! Always practice common sense and be safe!

TIPS:

☐ Don't talk to strangers. If somebody you don't know approaches you and asks you a question or tries to get a conversation going, walk away and ignore them.

☐ Always have a buddy with you if you go somewhere in the community (and make sure to get permission from your parents before you go).

☐ Have a way to contact your parents if you need help. A mobile device works great for this.

What about when you're home alone?

If you answer the phone and the caller asks if your parents are home, say they're busy or unavailable. Never say they're not home. If it's a bad guy on the other end of the line, he'll know that you're home alone!

If somebody knocks on the door, don't answer it. The same goes for the phone unless your parents say otherwise.

About the Author:

Born in 1974, Jess Walker is a Canadian author of children's and young adult literature. He writes fun, action-packed outdoor adventure stories mixed with the fundamental tenants of timeless life lessons aimed at building character, confidence, and safety awareness. He strives to inspire today's youth to get outside more (away from the screen) and make their own adventures happen.

Message from the Author:

When winter rolls around, make sure you get outside and enjoy it. If you have snow where you live, take advantage of it because it doesn't last long. Build a snow fort or a mean-looking snowman. Find your nearest hill and go sledding or skiing, have a friendly snowball fight (without the ice), make snow angels, try ice fishing, or lace up a pair of skates and hit the rink. Make your own adventures happen. Don't just wait for them to happen but make them happen. Feel it, experience it, be it!

More Books by This Author:

Walker Boys Series

Treasure Hunters

The Warrior Cup

Bigfoot

Like my book? Check me out on Facebook!

@ Walker Boys Books

Made in the USA
Las Vegas, NV
17 January 2024

84496547R00085